The lowlands of Moyne

Walleah Press
PO Box 368
North Hobart
Tasmania 7002 Australia
ralph.wessman@walleahpress.com.au

Cover image: Alison Girvan

ISBN: 978-1-877010-13-2

The lowlands of Moyne

Brendan Ryan

Acknowledgements

Thanks to the following people for their support and encouragement in the writing of the poems.

Barry Gillard, Alan Wearne, Robert Adamson, Lisa Gorton, A. Frances Johnston, Anthony Lynch, Ralph Wessman, Alison, Lucinda and Ruby.

My thanks to the editors of the following publications in which these poems first appeared.

Antipodes	'The lowlands of Moyne', 'Weeding: a love poem'
Australian Book Review	
States of Poetry 2	'A father's silences', 'Farmer's wife', 'Driving to Debating', 'The internet is poorer without you', 'The things they carry'
Australian Poetry Journal	'The Asbestos coast'
Cordite	'View of the new estates'
Eureka Street	'Dark Stars', 'Rollo's Road'
Island	'She was a Mugavin', 'Coconut workers', 'Brick kiln workers', 'Men I have worked with'
Meanjin	'Bacchus Marsh Road'
The Australian	'Driving with the West MacDonnells', 'The tools in his car boot'
Westerly	'Everything becomes metaphor', 'Lajamanu', 'Ampilatwatja'

'The Violin Player' was shortlisted for the 2018 Australian Catholic University Poetry Prize. 'The lowlands of Moyne' was also published in *The Best Australian Poems 2017* (Black Inc.).

Other collections by Brendan Ryan

Why I am not a farmer
A paddock in his head
A tight circle
Travelling through the family
Small town soundtrack

Contents

For Alison Girvan

Everything Becomes Metaphor

i.m John McKay

Looking down from the kitchen
into the valley's grainy darkness
I think of my neighbour who won't return
from hospital to imprint his side of the bed again.

A scattering of streetlights gives space
to his absence. Tiled roofs, poplars & magnolias
emerge to confirm the view. I live by what I see.
I remember my neighbour in his akubra

clambering along with his dog
giving me a startled wave, mouthing a wha?
as I curved past those days I failed to appreciate.
Trowelling beneath pebbles for kikuyu runners

I see what's beneath the urgency of the weekend —
damp clay clinging to the roots of weeds.
The boundaries of the backyard are
what I hunger for, where everything

becomes metaphor, enlivened and random
as hummingbirds drooping from blue Echiums.
Late evening light softens the corrugated zinc garden bed.
Only in memory does the voice of my neighbour begin to glow.

She was a Mugavin

She was a Mugavin before she was an O'Keefe.
They owned that farm on the Three Chain Road.
Her father was a great man, like salt and pepper
he was in everything. When he died, the son
took over, married that Gleeson girl.
What was her name?

How long have the McInernies been milking
at Boggy Creek? Well, she was a Murphy
before she married into the family. Her mother
was an O'Riordan, good people, her father was cranky,
drank the farm away. She gave him her name
and never looked back, reared nine kids
kept her health, sang up the front at Mass.
Like her mother she was known
by two initials on their cheque book.

There was a woman who kept her name
once she was married. She'd insert
her maiden name between brackets
like a correction to what had happened
after her father had given her away.
Once taken, it's hard to go back on a name
like the woman who was a Croft before
she was a Delaney before she became an O'Connor-
each name another point of departure.

Lajamanu

Wild brumbies complete their dawn ritual —
clattering through town chased by dogs.
The music of their hooves on the bitumen
reverberating, taking me down
into the earth.

Satellite dishes in the scrub angling
to capture the sun. Metallic flowers
that could be straight out of Gattaca.
I take photos to make sense of the land.
Nearby, the shack of a former abattoir.

A posse of dogs slink round dusty corners
biting car wheels, nosing through rubbish by the side
of the road. Cross-bred mongrels keeping health clinicians
in cars beeping for an elder to make an appointment.
Dogs howling through the night, pacing
concrete verandahs, ears and tails raised.
Behind a chicken-wire mesh fence
my senses twitching.

A 4WD on bricks, foam mattresses
outside houses, families spreading a
loose circle under a tree. Kids playing
basketball on a concrete court until dark.
Boys taking turns to dink each other on the handlebars.
What's your team? they ask, brushing my hand,
my arm, understanding by feeling
what I struggle to ask.

Four skin names in the community.
Walpirri people moved from their land
for a mine. In Gurrindjiri country, yawning children
line up for breakfast at the school canteen.
A sign on the supermarket door- *children
will not be served during school hours.*
I watch the boys training barefoot on a red gravel oval.
Light softens with the memory
of kicking a footy at the end of a school day.

The town is ringed by boundaries —
my expectations, spinifex, signs for men's land.
A dusty gravel patch where people camp for sorry.
A dried creek bed twists with its history
on the edge of town. The Wet
has left an upturned shopping trolley
encased in mud. In dusk light
where grasses seem to talk,
I walk with a stick that's like holding
a question, holding a look
I'm never sure will be returned.

At Katherine Gorge, an English mother stands
chatting to another woman in singlet, shorts and ponytail.
Her voice ripples across the viewing platform
as other tourists sit, shuffle, step around for the view.
*Darwin was dirty, I mean Aborigines everywhere.
I was in the supermarket when this Aboriginal woman
with a full load of shopping pushes through the self-serve
without paying and they're on welfare!*
The woman nods in affirmation. I sit
unable to not listen, wondering should I
intervene. I look away to the colours of the gorge
slipping from ochre to deep red.
The woman's frustration — measured,
articulate, defiant and the quiet that fell
when nobody on the platform spoke.

Dark Stars

After tea, I'd stand on the gravel lane beside the farm house,
look up to the scattered arguments of the Milky Way
stretching across our paddocks towards Naringal.

They were cities in the sky, gatherings of speckled light
giving shape to the dark that was never far from me.
The lights of other houses two paddocks away

reminded me there were other lives caught out by darkness.
When the silence outside the house was infiltrated
by the sound of cows pulling at grass, the heavy plod

of their hooves, or a snort or two I was reassured.
Yet when the cows weren't near the house
I'd imagine presences, shapes or shadows

appearing from beneath the cypress trees that towered
over the back yard. I'd turn to the glow of the kitchen
its yellow walls, smell the smoke from the chimney

and consider these paddocks I called home.
Like the stars that have collapsed into Black Holes
the darkness of the country night was always out there.

It lived in my dreams, had become a shadow unfurling
across paddocks. It was the depthless black
I dropped into during those falling dreams.

I kept it at bay with the company of brothers and sisters
and later learnt to accept it as that space between dusk and dawn.
On winter nights, when the world closed down early

the darkness was palpable, close and continuous.
It was the intimacy of a threat, the anger beneath a voice
the place where violence abandons you.

Each night the dark returned
I looked up to that spray of light,
those dark stars pulsating like a galaxy taken fright.

The lowlands of Moyne

Mud darkening the stories
what's passed down

utterances, quips
a way of looking at fences

the dark stretches
a scattering of bricks where a dairy was.

Farmhouses facing narrow back roads
wrecks of Commodores dumped in cape weed

beside rusted sheds. Heavy country you could
fatten a bullock with. A mother into farm politics

and the boot-deep mud around her dairy.

There were three brothers who drank day and night
until they killed themselves.

A mother who burned her house down
before leaving her husband.

A house with a green roof
fifteen kids came out of.

Children walking barefoot through John's Bush
stealing fruit from Faulkner's fence
after getting the cuts in a one-teacher school.

Stories the paddocks give up
like bits of pipe, old whiskey bottles.

Stories that go right back there
to a baby being brought home in a fruit box

a boy cutting thistles for one and six,
a girl walking away from the smell of onions

to a rail canteen at Spencer Street.

Once a week a draught horse pulls a car by rope
through water-logged paddocks.

A family of thirteen
cramped and grinning before Mass

slide around behind the horse
hauling them out of their rain-soaked bog.

In the days before electricity
my father said it was like skiing in mud.

The Violin Player

1

She relaxes into the rhythms of her bow, tapping her toes
to Uncle Bill swapping between accordion and
mouth organ; a Killarney reel in a damp country kitchen

she will hum on a bus to the dances
glancing at paddocks, stone crosses of the cemetery
a laughter-charged crowd bound for Saturday night at the Temperance Hall.

She knits her way through baby jumpers
casting on, knit and purl, casting off while a sister
takes the lead with the talk, the cooking.

The smell of the onion harvest on her brother's hands
she absorbs along with his talk of pruning roses,
of looking for an empty honey jar to take

to the Swinton's sale. She has learnt to listen

2

sitting in the back seat of a gold Holden Kingswood
in the Younger's department store car park.
Thick-rimmed glasses, silver necklace, pearl earrings

she smiles at the stories my mother gives her —
Uncle Dick in the city, the term I have just finished
the leather seats, her old person smells, gaps

in the talk my mother looks at me to fill.
The hours she wades through, unaccompanied
until her brother and sister return

with brown shopping bags, loaded and particular
while she turns to afternoon sun warming
her passenger window, the local fear of doctors

has rendered her sightless

3

sitting by the window of a front room. She listens
to cousin-talk of marriages, clearing sales,
the 1946 floods when she saw the river rise

above sheds, leaving piles of snakes writhing in its wake.
She will never marry or endure a long-term relationship.
Consigned to her favourite stool

memorizing her way to the bedroom, bathroom
how winter sun strikes round a country room,
the authority of her sister, the cunning of her small-time

farmer brother, who would never make a will for fear
of dying. A sister who could once swing a bow, smiling.
Each time I trudged through the car park to the Kingswood

I carried questions about darkness I would never ask her.

A Father's silences

Were you with a girl at the footy?
My father asks while weighing down on a milker.
His large, freckled hand like a stone on the claw
of the machines draining a back quarter
of an old Jersey reluctant to give.
I lean against a post darkened and polished
by our shoulders. *No, I was just going*
for a walk. He looks at me, adds, *I saw you*
behind the trees. My mouth begins to dry
and my heart picks up its beat. *No, I was*
just going for a walk, I repeat. He shakes
his head, turns back to the cow's flank.
I escape into the holding yard
round up a flighty heifer for the bail.
When our eyes meet
I'm the first to look away.

2

One afternoon he drove me to Terang
to catch the Melbourne train. Early
and waiting, I was struggling to find
things to say. I looked to the red
brick station, the car park, the dash board,
the radio controls, the heater, the automatic
gear shift lever, found myself muttering
about weather while my father looked ahead
and sighed. A familiar, rising dread was catching
in my breath. *I've got to go,* I blurted.
There was five minutes to spare.

My father, looking away, said, *no, stay.*
We faltered with our talk until a whistle
could be heard. I watched him drive away,
slow as any country father who has dutifully
waited for the train, waited for words
to come between silences,
silences I am learning to cultivate
driving my daughters around with their friends
accepting my role, keeping quiet
to avoid eye rolls, cutting looks.
Listening to their pauses and laughter
I think of my father – his silences
were paddocks that hadn't been ploughed before
paddocks it's taken me years to relax in
paddocks I've kept returning to again and again.

Farmer's Wife

Cracks in the clay, locusts flittering over bleached stalks
a woman steals a look from a farm house kitchen window.

She married into the district, thin as a whisper
a woman who was summoned to the front rows at Mass.

Wind ripples through washing, paddocks of rye grass sway.
She gave up teaching to smile through luncheons, gatherings.

She made the small talk that fertilized a district.
This year's heifers flicking their tails from the shade of a sugar gum.

Like a rumour she slipped round her kitchen
school forms for children, his phone calls after tea.

Hoof prints shadowing a cattle trough
the farmer who couldn't stop clearing his throat.

A hard doer, priests warmed to him talking a district,
a footy club, the cranky bugger who got things done.

Cypress tree shadows, muddy corner cut by the tanker
he bought up land, kept his neighbours at a distance.

Nerves in her family, shadows beneath her eyes.
He warned her to behave, lay off the grog

she laughed him off. Sheets of corrugated iron
curling from a pigsty. The woman who never touched the CWA

the woman who dressed for his municipal heights,
who drank to his occasions, who stood on the edge

of his name in the paper. They found her in the shower.
The parting statement of a farmer's wife echoing round a district.

An Increase in Doubt

The strange sensation
                    of returning to a place of memories
dislocated by what has changed
what has remained.
                    The quiet of paddocks
I return to as if eating, cooking –
                    these soggy drains are a part of my thinking.

What's buried, what's held – even scraps of rusted tin and iron
can become cairns to a time
                    my parents bought the river flats
                    by sitting in front of the neighbours
                    in a hall,
outbidding them for six months of silence
a farmer refusing to wave from his ute
                    until ageing prevailed.

                    Blue smoke rises from green paddocks
winter light distilled, longed for
                    clarity after rain
after the memories have played out
there is the hum of insulators on a fence
                    patterns on water
collecting in a ditch, cows sniffing me out.
                    Mt Emu Creek algae less.
The water level up
                    the price of butterfat down.
                    A slight breeze loosens the ferns.

Someone is shooting.
                        A homely retort echoing across
the span and reach of river red gums
where a tree can spread out, be shaped by wind
its closeness to the creek.
                                    Nearby
the frayed branches of a chalk-dry gum tree.
The twisted arcs and hooks of its years
soon to collapse
                                        while the dry cows continue
feeding out, raising a tail beside a cattle trough.

Looking uphill from the river flats
along the cattle track that rises like an inflection
to a ridge curving against the sky
                        hay has been spread out in the shape of a tear
                        drop. There is
                        traffic-hush on a distant highway,
                        and an increase in doubt where returning
takes me.

The things they carry

The sound of the streets is the growl of purpose
the six am momentum of fathers and sons
running errands down the alleys and footpaths of a city.

A whine that spirals to a high-pitched roar.
Waves of scooters flowing like oil around taxis,
through roundabouts. Nobody has time for burnouts.

The things a scooter carries – families, teenagers texting,
sacks of grain, a wardrobe, two goats in a basket, a small cow,
whatever's necessary

in a country with a history of invasions;
there is no road rage, just polite chaos at roundabouts.
I carry my ignorance, my Australian assumptions

where fall-out from the American War lingers
with genetic disorders, a man with deformed limbs
drags himself across a busy road. Fathers

who fought with the Viet Cong pass their stories
on to sons who lead tours to jungle temples
while veterans wake up screaming at dawn

drink rice wine, beat their wives
until their grand-daughters break the circle
talking of abortions, suicides, inherited violence.

The elderly who survive sell lottery tickets from a gutter
while the faces of those who disappeared
we pay our admission price to,

like the massacre at Ben Tre that has become
a place off a back road nobody talks about
except those who are willed to keep returning

with loud opinions and a shoulder bag
weighted by memories of the jungle.
Each morning a rooster crows. A radio station

broadcasts by loud speaker to the streets
what the government is doing. Who is listening?
Like heavy surf, traffic pulsates

outside my hotel window. I look down
to women sorting through hessian sacks
at a rubbish-sorting depot. Other women

fold their histories into rice paper rolls,
sit at markets with a meat cleaver and a tray of raw chicken.
 Meanwhile, men sit on low plastic stools

or laze in hammocks, scrolling.
The things a driver carries smoking on a river barge
steering a path between water lilies,

between the intimacy a woman creates washing
her hair in a Mekong tributary
and the histories a country asks its people to bear.

The things a tourist carries —
a baby's face squashed against her mother's chest.
The father driving without a helmet

their four-year-old son holding on.
His eyes stray to mine as the lights change
I step out before the motorbikes.

Coconut Workers

Watch the man in his stained shirt
barefoot under the palms.

Adrift from younger workers
he manages a rhythm, a cigarette-

dangling-from-the-lip focus.
His lined face belies the strength

of his forearms, thrusting each coconut
onto a metal spike that is his altar.

Seven days a week he steps up to the spike
splits coconuts with the precision required

to not sever a wrist
in a country with no health insurance.

❧

Three elderly women sit cross-legged
in the dirt, cutting and polishing,

woollen gloves protecting
their fingers from a glancing, curved knife.

They smile for my iPad
as though on exhibit in their

daily work space. Nearby, teenage boys
sit on low plastic stools smiling

at the guilt I might feel.
Sweat glistens on their backs

as they ram their feet against
twigs and mud for leverage. Too poor

for an education, they scrape and hack
at their country's fruit for twelve hours a day.

&

Factory work in the tropics – no different
to a cheese assembly line in Allansford.

Routine, repetition, incentive pay
I was able to walk away from the smell

of cheese off-cuts. Here, a loaded river barge
with two eyes painted on its bow,

finds a rhythm in its twice-daily return,
freighting coconuts to the known world.

Brick kiln workers

dozing in hammocks, scrolling on iphones
too far from home to return to,
they speak a language I don't understand
light incense, pray to a brick God
for twelve U.S dollars a day.

An arch doorway opens into the cathedral
quiet of the kiln. After cooling, the kiln
is emptied brick by brick sliding
down a metal chute where I watch
a man catch and twist, reminding me
of grabbing hay bales from the top of a loader –
the type of work that keeps you mongrel,
hurling bricks to an elderly woman
who scrambles to wheelbarrow them away.

When I was a brickie's labourer, I cut
my palms on the edges of bricks, wore
brick dust on my jeans, found a way
to keep fit without going to the gym,
but I didn't know how to make a brick.
I didn't know that the workers' children
scampering around the brick stacks
would have their futures mapped
by learning how to catch a brick.
I didn't know that a brick shaped
from the mud of a river was something
to hold, and in turn be shaped by,
like an iphone.

Men I have worked with

The timber worker who looked me in the eye
and said he wanted to understand his mother.

The father who wore white overalls and a hairnet
operating the cheese guillotine for forty years.

The quietly spoken manager who took a long lunch,
called me into the office and sacked me.

The man who ordered a pie, a sav in batter
and beat me in table-tennis each lunch time.

The man who talked with a rollie in his mouth.
The man who talked to himself while picking lemons.

The saw sharpener who gave every tool a place
and tried to give me words of advice.

The man who slept in his bath
when he couldn't find his bed.

The man I caught having a bong behind a stack of flitches.
The man with the DTs running off-cuts through a circular saw.

The short man with the large voice
who allowed me a coffee cup after three months probation.

The man who argued with his father, the owner
of the business, then walked away, shaking his head each day.

The man who introduced me at after work drinks
to a man who was the bloke to see if you wanted someone killed.

The man who paid for my long lunches
but couldn't always pay wages.

The man who sacked me after a morning's work
because I wanted to stack sports equipment my way.

The man who watered down clear spirits behind the bar
to conceal the bottles of vodka and gin he was giving to friends.

The barman who gave me dirty looks when I caught him
kissing women in the alleyway behind the Bar.

The man who smoked and swore through an interview.
The Principal who stepped aside from my interview to take a call.

The man I returned to three times to ask for my old job back
and who still didn't give it to me.

The man who wears shorts in winter, rocks
on the balls of his feet, stands with his legs apart.

The men who sit at a staff table with other men
waiting for someone to begin talking about sport.

The man I learnt to build barbed wire fences with
and the man who has taught me to take them down.

Rollo's Road

A holloway into the past
we drove cattle on. A road
that dips into the memory
of a wooden bridge scorched by bushfire.

Sliver of blue sky,
narrow strip of patched bitumen
threading a line between gum trees
leaning in to kiss each other.

Either side of the trees
muddy runs of dairy paddocks.
Like a lemming, I am pulled
to this tunnel of shade, this stretch

of bush to be held in, scuff my boots
amongst the ferns, a faded Jack Daniel's can,
pale scimitar of bone. Is there anything
so intoxicating as a quiet road

that makes a racket within me?
Is there anything that a memory
can't hollow, give passage to
moments gone wobbly beneath towering gum trees.

Bacchus Marsh road

For Peter Carey

An abattoir
a gun club, two prisons
rusting fences, leaning box posts
kangaroo bones.

Locusts, cracks in the clay
crumbling stone wall fences
a plough, a tray truck for sale.
milky summer haze.

Piles of rocks under trees
cars emerging from mirages
a mangled fox centre of road
paddocks stretching to the Brisbane Ranges.

Signs for Anakie
horse studs, empty dams, spindly trees
cars overtaking on corners
reasons for a novelist to leave.

The Princes Highway

1

I dreamt where the road could take me.
From two miles deep in the paddocks

I studied the intermittent flow of cars
listened to the wind-blown hush of traffic.

A one-mile stretch of highway became a stage
I was continually turning back to

checking to see if the twentieth century still existed.
I could squint and recognise milk tankers

from our back paddock, yet I always ended up
staring at Boo Boo Clark's farm.

2

This is the road that cuts through the heavy quiet of paddocks
a battered road that drags you through memory,

through the stories I have inherited
dips and bitumen ruts of the talk worn bare.

I plug into the spaces between white lines
an image of home I've spent a life escaping from.

In 1933, Nanna hitched rides with truckies
to visit a daughter at St Vincent's stricken with T.B.

A year later, she hitched a ride back from the city
up front in the hearse for 250 kilometres.

Somehow the highway passed through me
like an experience that drains without epiphany,

like the quiet that a woman endured
bringing her daughter home to the country

this slash of bitumen that funnels me deeper
into a family's song, beckoning.

Ampilatwatja

I drive a red sand highway into blue sky
through the scrub of Utopia
where stark white gums shiver and glow.
I never know what the road will offer.
I misjudge potholes, pass shredded tyres
termite mounds darkening like gravestones,
the torched shell of a car.
Here the language is Alyawarr
I wait in the quiet after muttered comments
trying to comprehend the raucous laughter,
the downward gaze that won't admit me.
My questions are cursory, glancing
as ash being scraped from a roo tail.
I spend my days watching
locals sitting on cars, chatting.
I make up answers to my questions
walking past car wrecks in back yards
reminding me of farmers' sons
who parked each successive crashed car
in a house paddock, storing them for spare parts.
I read of walking this country
that sings between red dust roads,
of explorers, missionaries and songlines.
I see teenage girls barefoot pushing prams
a donkey pulling at weeds.
At the bush tucker workshop
older women sit around nonchalantly
drawing plants with acrylic texta.
The ease of their lines, how they recline
smile, mutter, sigh. It could be a CWA gathering.
I walk the gravel streets trailed by dogs

and the judgements I didn't expect to begin.
Here, where a low sun sets fire in smoky light
I sit on a concrete porch waiting
for the questions to kick in.

Driving to debating

Lights over the rail yards are sparklers
that never die down. *Every day
is a drug test day.* All that's left at Ford
is the security lights, shadows on the pedestrian overpass.
George Pell is refusing to leave Roma
where girls were once named after their fathers
who could, if so desired, sell them at fourteen
into slavery. George is obstinate
as the music I listen to is old, out of date,
timeless. George is of a time that haunts
like a rash, of looking the other way,
of a justice that dare not be spoken of.
      The brake lights of cars have become
pulses within my thoughts. Tim Buckley
launches into Sweet Surrender – the epic
confession to bruised love I never tire of.
The shuttered weatherboards of Norlane
give way to the spindly trees of Corio
as empathy hardens like a row of bollards.
George pauses to compose before a camera,
to restate his innocence while families in Ballarat
attend funerals, not Mass. Flash of the golden arches,
lurid glare of a Caltex, George is immovable as The Sphinx
on Thompson Road, unforgiving as a red arrow.
I turn right into the darkness of School Road.

View of the New Estates

Instead of church spires, mobile towers
offer reception on treeless ridges.
A scattering of solar panels glints
amongst the tessellated greys and browns.
Trees are kept to an acceptable height.
Each garden holds a two-year history
of yuccas, cordylines or three weeping birches.
No eucalypt spreads its arms above the spouting.

Only on the fringes are the houses let loose
spreading like rumours into paddocks
where grids of bitumen are gouged
out of clay, streetlights inserted, kerbing set
acres of clover and rye grass transformed into Ridge View —
a lifestyle to walk through to a map of the future
rendered in display homes and flickering wide-screens.
Perhaps the finest suburban view
is seen from a circling flight,
a mosaic of ochre and charcoal tiled roofs
reminding us how hardened the landscape seems.

The asbestos coast

The bellies of clouds lowering over a town
of asbestos shacks, weekenders with boat drive-
throughs,
of dirty Commodores and out-sized dogs
deserted streets waiting for summer to happen,
where the wind is so strong, tourists stumble
to gain a foothold,
where men nurse a stubby on the golf course
for breakfast
where locals greet you with a wave, a grunt
and hobble forward, stooped as a ti-tree
to buy the papers,
where dairy farmers elevate themselves
with a house by the beach,
while the Southern Ocean heaves against the limestone
of Massacre Point.

Through an upstairs window
the illusion of waves crashing over paddocks,
foamy waves rolling toward Rubbish Tip Bay —
a relentless reassurance of something
uncontained. Everything we've ever dumped
comes back to haunt us.

The Internet Is Poorer Without You

i.m Max Richards

Somehow you found the articles and poems
I needed to read.
Your key word searches driven by connection,
of passing it on.
Whether it be through the nodes of ADSL2
or the poetry of Heaney,
Murray, or MacFarlane's nature writing,
whether you be in Doncaster
or Seattle, or your shelves of books and manila folders
at La Trobe,
you were always passing it on.
Whatever you found for me on the internet,
I read as personal,
yet it was only after your death that I learned
I was one of the many,
scattered across the globe who received the news
you set before us.

I sent you all I had written, for you were a first reader —
forgiving, close,
a grammar stickler. Mostly your feedback confirmed
the work I had to do.
Sometimes poems were returned and broken up
into stanzas or quatrains
giving form to my ramblings. Your own poems arrived
almost daily-
light, diary entries of dogs, trees, squirrels, dream poems
of other poets,
the last outing with your mother
the words of a father

your tendency to be sombre yet playful
about dying.
Your poems grew into a life from '*an inarticulate and non-self-*
examining culture'.
The moments you left us.
The urge for the next poem may be all that a life writing poems
can teach us.
There is no absence like the days following an email of poems
sent —
to see if a poem breathes or dies.
Your replies were never late, sometimes within hours.
The warm, confiding voice
is still in my head. The teacher who would rather exclaim
in wonderment than complain in negativity.

I was on holiday when I heard you had been knocked down
by a car,
your dog refusing to leave your side.
Some hours after my last email, some hours
after I last thought of you,
the absence of its reply I am continually adjusting to.

Comfort

The idea of trouble receding
with the opening bars of the Theremin.
Joyce is in the kitchen bottling jars

of Medlar jelly, Barnaby and Troy
are sharing jubes
as they hurtle down a hedgerow lane.

Saturday night, all I want is three murders
clunky flashbacks and a feud
between landed gentry and village idiots.

Barnaby will be my moral guide, Troy
my bumbling conscience while I lose
myself to a montage of paddocks

thatched cottages, English faces weathered by drink.
The plots are *sheer lunacy*. Barnaby
bases his investigation on the gossip of locals,

slow pauses of memory, clues spelt out
through a woman's needling glance
and a flurry of strings. The first murder

slots into place and I subside from a day
of emails and forgetting student names.
Even though The News provides nightly

murders and home invasions, I prefer
watching a syringe being plunged into a stomach
from a distance. I know which spoilt daughter

of a wayward Lord is a red herring,
which spurned secretary is capable
of stabbing a friend in the neck.

It's what I've come to expect —
the terrors of the world held at bay by Barnaby.
Still, the murders pile up as the plot lines thin —

a man impaled on a plough in a barn
a missing person surfacing hog-tired and swollen
in the murky waters of a dam,

Security may be our chiefest enemy
but I like the comfort of having my fantasies
delivered, guaranteed. Barnaby's moral summaries

clarify and lull like a second whiskey.
His final quips to Troy of a dissolute family
'ripened by their own corruption'

restores the moral order I've been seeking
from the English villages of Causton, Midsomer Worthy —
local places I know, trust in, like Barnaby and Joyce

enriching their lives with Medlar Jelly,
while the Member for New England-
Barnaby Joyce learns to stew

in the hubris of his meddling.

Hinterlands

What do we feel when a parent is struggling
for breath, for traction on a footpath?
The pull of getting back to them

to change a dressing, clip their toenails.
The care that's unspoken oscillates
through the day – appointments, blister packs,

nagging thoughts. Past arguments settle
into their own terrain.
Things you no longer talk about

the way your parents could never lie,
now you are dropping by, calling over.
The parents who don't want any fuss

keep chocolates two years past their due date
and talk of funerals the way you talk of Netflix.
What you will do to keep them alive

in the now, amongst the talk, the paperclips,
unopened mail we never get to put away.
Words we've been meaning to share

but can't think of, like walking into a room
and second-guessing why you came there.
What we see when we read each other's glances

what we feel when we hold paddocks
leveling to the horizon, spaces
razored by memory –

the way grief sentences a man to repeat
the days of his mother's passing.
The talk that circles a death,

when each day becomes an event
to find change for the car park,
days thrown together like serviceable clothes.

I keep returning to gravel roads
somebody else is taking
past shadows from cypress trees

that pull dry cows the length of a paddock
to give birth in, muddy, protected spaces
no Display Home could conjure or promise.

Still, I gain shelter with late night calls
listening to recounts of their days
my voice rising above the remotes and shopping bags

recalling the names that will have them talking
dwelling in the stories that somehow become us,
the waking questions we want someone to reply to.

Intentionality

On the day the Prime Minister was knifed
a Manchurian pear tree was set adrift by a flurry
of white petals gusting across a weedy lawn
a woman holding a stop/go sign looked away
as cars passed her
two school girls walked out of a class room
shouting *I'm pumped for recess!*
a man ran along a footpath wearing a bulging
back pack and a worried expression
a magnolia tree cupped the day with its rose-wine petals,
I held a friend's baby and saw life sparkle in his eyes
a woman pushed her legs skyward
on a black rubber swing while her daughter
built a cubby from fallen branches beside her
a driver swerved through three lanes of traffic
and the new Prime Minister's ministry was assembled
within two days of his win

Weeding- a love poem

Couch grass, bindweed, dock and dandelion.
Each weed takes me back to earth
to the bending, the pulling, the constant work.

To weed is to love drifting off
to the smell of capeweed
in a winter paddock

long wavering heads of spear grass
on the river flats in summer,
tussocks that cut our fingers

Scotch thistles I hacked from the dirt
scrubby ferns I couldn't get enough of
stretches of blackberry where we hid dead calves.

Pigweed, Fat hen, oxalis and nettle.
kneeling before buttercups I think about
things I shouldn't think about.

The very plants I want to yank out
I'm finding ways back to love
sour sob, lantana, nut grass.

I pull out weeds to see where the day
has gone, a type of reverie like listening
to the radio outdoors, of doing one job

while attending to another, of returning
to milk thistle where the thinking gets done,
to weed is to love the plants nobody wants.

Dancing at the crossroads

They used to dance at the crossroads
polished heels sliding over gravel,
a left foot leading against the wind.
A bus kicking up dust between paddocks
took them to the Temperance Hall.
There's a photo of them at the Belle of the Ball:
eyes closed, her head on his shoulder
a woman nearby stifling a snigger.
A moment emblematic of the 1950s —
a mother who sat between them
on dates in the Vanguard.
Before children, before going out
an Evening Two Step on the Moyne Road.

Jonquils

When I visit this house
    ten children scrambled out of
        I think of jonquils

wavering in a winter breeze by the gravel lane.
    Their smells freshened
        by muddy paddocks

springers drooling bow-legged about to calve.
    I walk inside shouldering my absence
        from insignificant places —

where our rubber boots fell
    where we played sock footy
        where we knelt to pray

what we were doing when the phone rang.
    Somehow I've stepped into a lost country
        where the bedrooms have shrunk

the fireplace has been boarded up
    and the inhabitants have fled
        pursued by memories

they didn't want to own up to.
    The new island bench fails to update
        the kitchen where I poured

boiling water down a brother's back
    where ice blocks chunked through the night
        when the fridge was being defrosted

and where my mother gave a roomful of footballers
        the heave-ho
                after a premiership all-nighter.

The groan of the screen door has never left me
        nor the tea towels being flicked
                at bare legs.

Once a house has become a place
        to stare at paddocks from
                the laws of familiarity kick in,

like the way I still talk to my siblings
        as if we were ten. This is the house
                I've turned back to from the highway-

the distracted, departing look
        where I hope to claim some meaning
                from a paddock,

like the glimpse of my parents
        in the rear-view mirror
                the first time I drove away.

Yet a house in a paddock is all it ever was —
        temporal as the fragrance of jonquils
                wafting by the gravel lane each winter.

Tussocks and Ferns

Two men pulled up on the gravel beside the wooden milking shed.
The younger man was first out of the car. Squinting, he looked
to the land, then stepped toward a sagging barbed wire fence
as if having already made a decision. The older man
closed the car door, paused and surveyed what was before him.

There were thickets of two-metre high tussocks
skulls of tree stumps and long, wavering thistles
that grew in clusters as if they were a community in need of each other.
He let his eyes be carried further east
to what he imagined might be the boundary of the land.

There were stands of eucalypts, clumps of blackberry, a scattering of ferns.
The farm was comprised of four paddocks, so large
that the older man could barely run his eye along a fence line.
Apart from the trees, the only other upright object
was a windmill, it's iron flag as still as a cloud.

The younger man walked toward the herd of cows
standing in a huddle near a rusted gate.
It was like walking back in time to another era
before tractors and cars, in the time
of the bullock and dray, and before that time

to when locals walked the land, singing to it,
feeding on eels, settling down for a time by the creek.
The cows had been bought on credit and delivered
to the farm earlier that day; Jerseys, with a few Guernseys,
three Friesians. Cows that didn't know the land.

The leader cows were twitchy and nervous, glaring at the dirt
flare-eyed, in a suspicious manner. The younger man hollered
and lifted his arms as if they were wings until the herd
was gathering as one, hopping along a soft dirt track
toward the concrete yard of the dairy.

Thistles and weeds grew in the cracks of the yard.
The cows began to arch their backs and soon the dry,
darkened patches of concrete were washed by piss.
The younger man took in the smells and looked over
the cows' bony ridges. It was a moment where his decisions

were confirmed — the day he walked away from the factory
the night he talked with his wife about leaving their conite home
for a rundown weatherboard in the country
the farms that his father could never manage.
He was looking over the backs of cows to paddocks that could be his own.

There was no electricity and the dairy's engine
was powered by a petrol motor. The older man
poured some petrol in from a rusted container, pulled
the cord to start the engine. It coughed and gulped
like a beast reluctant to turn over.

Soon the engine was stuttering into life
and the rhythm of air being squeezed and expanded
sang its familiar song. The sound was a heart-beat
a pulse, a music both men had grown up with
a rhythm they had learnt to trust.

The dairy consisted of six wooden bails in a row.
A modest, yet common arrangement.
Each cow had to be coaxed and prodded forward.
Sometimes it took a shoulder behind a cow's rump;
sometimes it was the clap of a hand on a stomach or hip.

Once a cow was secured in the bail, her outer leg was tied back
by a leg rope which stopped the younger man from being kicked.
He squatted on a small wooden stool, rested his head against the cow's flank
breathed in its animal warmth. It was an intimacy
his factory job had never been able to provide.

Before the milking machines could be put on the cow
her teats were rubbed clear of dust, massaged, and washed
with warm water. Each teat was squeezed until
a fine jet of milk needled the concrete. The younger cows
stamped their feet and swished their tail as the machines

were swung beneath their udders. The high-pitched moan
of the machines was quickly silenced by the cups
sucking on each teat. While one cow was giving up
her milk, another cow was being guided towards the bail
to have her leg tied back, her teats washed.

There was repetition and ease to the milking.
The two men working side by side, muttering directions
sometimes grinning when a cow took fright.
There was muck and spilt water, the sour breaths
of cows waiting on the concrete of the holding yard.

The warm milk was pulled up from the machines
through thin steel pipes into a cool-room
where the milk followed gravity down over the ripples
of a metal water-cooler and along a galvanized pipe
into the unrefrigerated milk vat.

A simple process that was dependent on the temperament
of a nearby windmill to drag hard water from beneath the ground
and channel it through the cooler.
In one hour the herd had filled a quarter of the vat.
A winged agitator swirled the milk clockwise and then anti-clockwise.

The metal lid of the vat was kept closed as a fridge door
so that flies mostly hovered outside. The tanker driver
would arrive the next morning to take what had been given.
The younger man knew he couldn't argue
with what a Jersey could produce in marginal country.

Hungry country, the older man had said.
Country that hadn't been ploughed before.
They washed up and gazed at the herd filing back
into the paddock of waist-high tussocks. Already,
the younger man could see the paddock for what it was.

On the drive back to their families and lives
the two men stopped off at a pub to buy long necks of beer.
They sat in the bar wondering what they had just done
in that wild, rubbishy land. They were factory workers
who toiled through rotating shifts packaging cheese

with their background in farming lodged like a stone in their shoe.
The older man had toyed with cows until his betting on the nags
helped him to appreciate the regularity of a factory pay cheque.
He knew the risk the younger man was taking.
He thought of the fence line that he had stared at

when he first saw the land. Only now he realized,
he had been looking into a mirage; the watery distances
a back paddock can conjure in a farmer. For years,
he had thrown his own money at horses and lost.
He wasn't sure he could watch the younger man gamble

for the sake of his wife and five kids. And yet,
the younger man was grinning. Here was his chance
to walk out of a factory that had softened his skin for seven years.
He had no money; only a wild idea that a herd of cows
could fill a vat from a paddock of tussocks and ferns.

These people

Sometimes I shared a compartment with students
decked out in green hair, black lipstick, traces of leather.
Nobody spoke. We had our magazines and books
crossed our legs, rocked a shoe, found ourselves

vindicated by the night flashing by farm porches.
Our lives in transit, each of us too anxious
to open up, swaying to dangerous thoughts.
Only the elderly made eye contact, asked

who I knew in Warrnambool or Terang,
yet my eye was on the alternative types
stepping from the train with their nose rings,
ripped jeans and studded belts

being hugged by mothers wearing Sloppy Joes
who reached up for a peck on the cheek
before announcing who was getting married,
who was expecting, who had died.

These punk outsiders who had left the country in a hurry
who didn't fit in at Blue Light discos
with their sharp looks and long coats,
who didn't want to work in a bank or abattoir

or drink with the same people singing along
to Dr Hook or *Bye Bye Miss American Pie*.
These people who could smell the country
in the way people spoke, in the TV ads

for tractors, *Nilverm*, Agricultural Field Days.
These people who kept their return tickets
closely guarded as the secrets they knew
they would have to one day confront

and who would later say by way of apology
I grew up in the country, as if an apology
could ever explain waking to paddocks from a bedroom,
the ineluctable pull of the city on the Sunday night train home.

Patches of concrete

The patches of concrete in a three-metre square holding yard
of a walk-through dairy are the details necessary

to tell of a history of Jerseys clustered and waiting
to be milked. Each patch

was a country in a map suggesting India,
Uruguay, most of Alaska.

I studied the countries and knew
they represented something that located me

like the way my father stamped his rubber boots
on the concrete while eyeing off the last cows filing up the track.

There were places within the concrete
I would never tell my father about

distances that became familiar over time
dreaming places land-locked by what they contained.

Like many sons, my father is often just out of reach
sniffing around in the machinery shed

casting an eye over where the windmill was
while I brood over patches of concrete.

This is what it is like to be unhinged by the familiar —
every rail is rusted

lone gum trees have collapsed yet the wind
still shaves the side of a cypress tree plantation.

We drive out to the farm for something to stare against
to be owned by what we end up talking about.

My father says coming out here is like going to Mass —
you feel better about yourself.

Each time I pause before the holding yard
tufts of grass are sprouting in the cracks

I listen to the tap tap tapping of the electric fence meter box
and I realize once again, what it is like to be mapped.

Tainted Waters

The sewage from our dairy gurgled
into an open channel that spilled
into a larger drain the bulls
used to rub their shoulders against.
Ibis picked in the spongey grass
more than once I copped a sockful
wading through in rubber boots.
The drain we buried kittens in
opened out into a meander, tainted waters
snaking through the river flats,
before Mt Emu Creek accepted the run-off
from ours and other dairies. It was
a way of making our presence felt —
our drains coursing with cowshit and fertilizer
choking the river with algae, killing off eels
our very own muck following its nose to the sea.

Driving with the West MacDonnells

Flecks of bloodwood and mulga scattered over red sand
I long for your sharp retorts, their familiar force.

I'm driving at 130ks with a mountain range
curling like a breaking wave, its oxide-stained

rocks bearing the blood that light gives.
The bitumen is straight and unrelenting.

The range on my left keeps pace, a story
of red shale packed tight as bricks.

Even though we are two states apart
your morning voice is in my head,

resident, as the high-pitched squeal you give
to dog videos. I'm paying attention to what's due

thinking of you running from clients to supermarkets,
to music lessons, the K-Mart drop-off.

I drive to be alone with you
while four teenage students shout

along to Selena Gomez's *Me and My Girls.*
Here landforms are tectonic, momentous

I'm quietened by the ranges' telling presence
the lemony light of spinifex and ghost gum.

I'm learning to trust the thoughts this road shifts
how absence brings the idea of you closer

knowing what it feels like to stand beside you
in a crowded room, I'm never lost

but now, weathered by distance from your voice
I look to the mountain, this flatness announcing itself.

Forgiven

I have never experienced such devotion.

Within two metres of me, she lays in the sun
her midnight coat, glossy and warm. A low pant
emanates. She raises an eyebrow when I call her,

clambers to her feet, sidles against the cool
of a retaining wall, scratches her back against
low shrubs before slumping to her haunches

watching me oil the faded woodgrain of a garden chair,
a job I've been stretching out over summer days –
rubbing back worn edges, sandpaper tearing at the creases.

She is a thief who steals for love.

Yesterday while I was out, she stood up to prise
the paint brush and rag from the laundry bench.
This morning I discovered them heaped on the deck

just like the glossy travel guides she dragged through a dog-flap
and onto an outdoor table. She rests her jaw on whatever I touch
brushes her wet nose against my leg after work,

dances, circles, runs into garden statues the moment
a dogstick appears. Muscles tensed, jaw dripping
we make eye contact, all is forgiven.

Heifer wearing a fence post

When she lowers her muzzle to the clover
the post chafes her neck, swings against her shoulder.
No more than a wooden spacer tied to a loop
of cyclone wire strung round her neck.
She wears her post like a cross, bears its weight
its annoying shape for the days needed
to corral a wayward heifer.
Aversion therapy, designed to stop her twisting
through fences, the lone heifer who discards
the herd to freely wander. The same process
we use to justify drowning kittens in a hessian bag,
whacking crippled calves on the head with an axe
watching the cattle buyer jab an electric prodder
into cows reluctant to climb into the darkness
of a cattle truck. In moments such as these
we separate ourselves from the animals,
realise who we are to detach ourselves
from the fear of the cow we are selling.
Like chaining a dog or dehorning a bull
our aim is to contain something wild,
rebellious, a heifer who will twist her neck
to pull at rye grass on the neighbour's boundary,
her fence post bowing the barbed wire
before she pulls back, snickets of orange fur snagging
She learns to wear her post
as a sailor wears an albatross. Other heifers
keep their distance, shun her affliction.
Each time she shakes her head at flies
the post knocks against her side like a voice
reminding her to pause before fences.

Dehorning

Twisting the metal nose pincers is a job reserved
for older brothers. Once the pincers are clamped
onto the septum, the cow's head is pulled forward,
twisted to one side, its shoulders heaving against the crush.
The galvanised reo shudders and jars
to each kick, each sudden arse-end shift.
It's simply a matter of clutching the pincers
the way a water skier latches onto a tow rope.
My father slides the blades down
over the curved horn. He leans back, draws
the steel arms together until they kiss.
A severed horn is caught, turfed into a hessian bag.
Soon there will be a pile of blood-smeared horns
some warm, smelling of cow's breath, rank hair.
'Twist the head the other way,' my father shouts.
Blood needles from the stump, arcing
across my father's face, his leather apron.
Crack! Another horn falls into the bag
dogs are sniffing towards. It's a progress
of sorts, protecting the herd from stomach gouges.
My father's mood tightens as the horns pile up.
I look back to marrow pulsing in the skull
the swivelling eye, glare from an animal trapped.
She snorts froth from her muzzle, bellows and groans,
quietens the moment the gate is swung.
There is blood on my shirt, in my hair
in muddy puddles around our rubber boots.
Some cows bolt up the track, others trot
shaking their heads at blood trickling down
into the powdery cattle track dirt.
We squirt some liquid onto the wounds

to staunch the flow, but most cows
escape from the crush bloodied as punch-shocked boxers
their bullying hierarchy zapped, heads lowered
as if they had escaped the smells of war.
Within a day their scarlet stumps will dry.
No longer will they spook when they see the crush
or hop back sniffing dirt beside a stray horn dropped.
The real test of brothers is dehorning a bull –
its horn thick as a fist, close to a ton of beef
squeezed into a cattle race. It takes two
to twist a Hereford's head into position.
The grip on the pincers, locked, here is a beast
that quickens voices, turns each pull of the septum,
in to some type of family emergency.
Both horns off, we leap back away from the crush
once the bolt is lifted, not even fences are safe.
My brothers hang on the looks from our father.

The smell of a paddock

Driving a tractor around a paddock concentrates the mind.
Whether it be pulling a set of discs, smudgers or harrows
large rocks, ditches and skull stumps need to be driven around.
The curves, Buddhist in style, lead you back into the centre
for you are turning a paddock over, twisting in the tractor seat
the way a parent twists to adjust a toddler's seat belt watching
loose dirt fall away from you until the taste of the paddock
is in your mouth the way dust from a gravel road seeps through
a jammed ute window. A dry, consuming smell mixed
with diesel fumes sweeping back at you.

I follow the line of darkened soil where the harrows have run
watching sparrows flit from a furrow. When there was a head wind
I drove in a compromised position to avoid swallowing dust
except dirty air blocked my nose, closed my eyes. Cross-winds
gave me breathing space yet sometimes the wind just skittered
and swirled around the blue Leyland while the discs clanged behind
like an orchestra tuning up.

In summer, the mix of heat, dust and diesel fumes lulls me
into a sleep. I pull up to rest my head on the steering wheel
making sure the tractor is in a gully or down the back paddock,
somewhere out of sight so my father standing at the back door
scanning the horizon for a rising cloud of dust might not be
disappointed. Yet tractor work was a job my father was bound
to praise; days of back-juddering routine to sew turnips and rape,
layers of topsoil billowing towards Heaven, the meditative calm
of steering a Ferguson while chewing over unearthly paddock thoughts.

A harrowed paddock is rich in smells, of wind and loose dirt.
I step down from the tractor and walk across the soft ridges
to simply breathe in the earth. I scuff my boots over a furrow
and like a fantasy, dust pirouettes above me. The smell
of the paddock is the smell of the farm; of teenage isolation,
fence lines that never waver, smells that memory misses,
waves of clay furrows, tilled park land. Layer upon layer of memory
unfolding the turbulence of the ground. Somehow I've managed
to subdue forty acres, tame its wildness, know its spaces intimately.
I know its corners the way a woman knows her husband's evasions
yet I have lost the paddock I've ploughed and found what it means
to be harrowed driving in second on a half-throttle, dust and diesel
fumes in my face. I cling to where the paddock takes me tracing
a line of darkened soil with the smell of dust following me
like a threat.

White butterflies

White butterflies quivering
over a paddock of turnip and rapeseed.
The afternoon beginning to stretch into a loop
of undriven thoughts.
Golden hues of round bales, stacked, lined up
leaving expanses of stubble to tease the eye
to render distances personal.
How to take in the view you keep returning to.
By a gravel road, flies, a clump of blackberry
straggly branches of towering pine trees
their shadows lengthening into memories.
Always the burnished light catching the eye
like windscreens on a distant highway.
Redgums curving with a creek, unwavering
as the family farms you grew up with,
those certainties, ways of looking at paddocks –
now there are widows living on in farm houses
the road I caught the school bus on
haunted by rusting mail boxes for the McKinnons,
Healeys and Finnigans. What I thought I knew
has amounted to a quiet back road the world
can easily ignore.
What is definite is the land rising by degrees
to a mountain, resolute at 330 metres –
a contention to argue with
a shadow that quickens the breath
no matter the times you look and look again
it becomes the landform you dream against.

Incident on South Valley Road

Past five of a Saturday
                    driving my girls home from drama
past the thwock of balls on the tennis courts
past the bottle shop and Squeakies's car wash
                                round the corner
towards home.
A topless man, barefoot, paces the footpath
a look on his face that spells danger.
                            I recognise him from the week before
shouting at a woman in the street
A moment I had wondered
                        should I step in, say something.
He was pointing his finger at her.
She was a distance away, behind a car
                        shouting back.

I drive up the hill, past the nursery
                        follow him in the side rear-view mirror
watch him lurch onto the road
and dive into the side of a car driving towards him.
                        His head bounces off the bumper
the driver stops.
I pull over, tell the girls to stay in the car
                        run down to where the man is laying
face down, like a chalk outline
                        on a gleaming Saturday afternoon.

Blood pools around his head.
He is breathing fast, making low, guttural sounds.
                        I try to calm him, know
I shouldn't move him or touch his skin.
                        Heat radiates from his body.
The sound he makes is a mixture of anger
and disappointment.
Other people run over, an ambulance is called.
A woman shouts, 'I'm training to be a nurse.'
She returns to her car for a towel.
                    The driver who hit him
                    paces in circles, shaking his head
                    repeating his words.
We wait for the ambos, recount the event
from seven perspectives.
                        A man in tracksuit pants head-butting
                        the side of a car on a gleaming
Saturday afternoon.

He turns over, a gash to his temple, bruising
to the side of his back.
                        He looks at me, stunned, in another
world
and despite my pleas, gets up
walks back to his Salvo brick veneer unit
that fronts the footpath.
                        I follow him to the door, all the while
talking, trying to keep him occupied
                        from knives and their possibilities.
The lounge has a TV, couch
reeks of cigarettes and sweat.
                        He stumbles in circles, glaring.
I am out of my depth and know it.
                        He looks at me, faintly registering, asks
                        Can you kill me?

I look away, embarrassed
before he walks out to the footpath
where the witnesses contain him.
                    More cars pass, the ambos arrive
shepherd him inside, leaving seven people to talk about
what we couldn't believe
until we run out of things to say
watching the blood stain on the road
tennis games continuing
sidelong glances from other drivers.

The tools in his car boot

Hammers, a set of screwdrivers, a file,
a stillson, spanners. For the jobs he might do —
fetching a shifter to replace a worn bathroom tap washer
gripping a burred thread with a lock-nut wrench.
Repairs he can make sense of
unlike his visits to the Memory unit
where his wife misses days
entranced by the poster of the man
with rosy red cheeks and white bushy beard.
He brushes strands of hair from her face
sponges her lips with water. He has learnt to let go
of her talk of harvesting, smoko, cordial in a foam esky.
Ageing, she says, *they say that getting older
is called ageing, fancy that.*

He pauses at a rural city's roundabouts
picks up a lotto ticket, breaking up
the day the way milking cows closed it.
He looks out from what was their ground floor unit
to bitumen, kerbs, not a paddock in sight.
He looks for jobs that could be done
what his wife wants, talks of
the doctors say they can't fix.

He keeps to the routines he can trust
knowing the woman she was
could be within reach today
and how a Phillips-head screwdriver
can give form to a shelf
how a claw hammer and a box of galvanised
staples can dress a fence,

how some days are better kept close to the chest
like a set of tools wrapped in a grease-stained cloth
in the boot of a car.

Home

Light suffers to soften, thin ghost gums begin to glow.
I'm sitting on a concrete verandah bedazzled by flies
humming along eyelids, up my nose, in ears, swallowed.
People cruise in dusty Commodores towards the shop at low speed.
Families of women and children scuffing down narrow bitumen streets.
A woman sits in the dust outside her house, a canvas she is working on
spread out before her. A posse of dogs recline in the dirt, wreathing her.
There is washing hanging over fences, the darkness of front doors, engine parts,
kids riding in the back of a ute from the shop.
All morning, council workmen have been tending to the bitumen
their patches higher than the road that trails off into red dust.
Some kids walk home from the shop with super-doopers.
A boy plucks a caterpillar from a host of weeds.
Six pm, bands of light blue and dusty pink above the horizon.
Someone is playing instrumental Country music to the street
a slow, mournful loop that reminds me of Gurrumul,
yet the night unsettles with kids' high-pitched voices, a dog barking,
streetlights sparkling in the dirty light, and further, in the gathering darkness
orange glow of a campfire. The mood after a long talk about country
the chasm that widens between the South and the North
when a consultant walks into a classroom looking for a pointer.
Six-thirty, security lights of the verandah blink on, notes of a steel guitar
blend with a light breeze that lifts another evening.
I think of Carl Strehlow's final journey along the sandy, silt flats of the Finke
his swollen, Lutheran body shuddering over shale and gibber plains
the man regarded as a rock, beginning to crumble. No God could save him.
Thy will be done, his son Theo intones walking behind a buggy being hauled
by donkeys towards crimson sand hills in 1920. Meanwhile
a nine-year old boy with dirty, matted hair and a borrowed school shirt
weaves a soccer ball, barefoot, between his opponents' ankles.
He feints, stutters, races over bindis, gravel and weeds of a school pitch
managing the ball with his toe, matted hair flowing, slipping between legs

with the delicacy of something missed, something balanced, something that lingers like the notes of an Hawaiian country guitar hanging like dust from the growl of a white Commodore, brake lights flashing to the howls of dogs, turning in towards home.

Notes

Home
The poem was partially inspired by a reading of Journey to Horseshoe Bend, TGH Strehlow, Giramondo Classics, 2015. The following lines are taken from the book:
thy will be done p213,
the man regarded as a rock, beginning to crumble p213.

Heifer wearing a fence post
The term *aversion therapy,* was inspired by the short story, Kill or Cure, Cate Kennedy, Dark Roots, Scribe,

Driving to Debating
The Sphinx is a hotel on Thompson's Road, North Geelong which has a sculpture of The Sphinx of Giza on its roof, so that the roof becomes the Sphinx.

Intentionality
This poem refers to the abrupt sacking of Malcolm Turnbull as Prime Minister in 2018 by the Liberal Party.

Dancing at the Crossroads
This poem refers to the tradition held in Australian rural areas and in Ireland of couples meeting at crossroads in the country for a dance. Sometimes the dances were a prelude to going out; sometimes they were a semi-regular informal dance held at crossroads in the country. The photo referred to in the poem is of my parents, pre-marriage, pre-ten children.